How to Hold Scissors

Insert your thumb into the smaller opening of the scissors. Then insert your index finger and middle finger (in some cases, your ring finger as well) into the larger opening.

Base of the scissors

★ The base of the scissors is where the two blades meet.

★ Use scissors with rounded points and edges.

Thumb
(Right before first joint)

Index finger

Middle finger

★ Use child-sized scissors that are easy to open and close.

How to Use Scissors

When using scissors, the elbow of the arm that is holding the scissors should be touching the body at the waist. Scissors should be held straight out from the body, and the paper should be held perpendicular to the scissors.

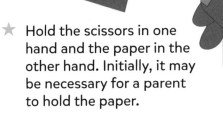

★ Insert the paper deep into the scissors. Open and close the blades repeatedly to cut a straight line.

★ Hold the scissors in one hand and the paper in the other hand. Initially, it may be necessary for a parent to hold the paper.

T0057299

CAUTION

- Always carry scissors by the handle, CLOSED, and blades DOWN.
- When handing scissors to someone, hold the CLOSED blades in your hand and pass them off with the HANDLE OUT.
- Don't cut anything but paper with scissors.

- Always sit down when using scissors.

- Don't touch the sharp edge of the scissor blades.
- Don't point scissors at living things.

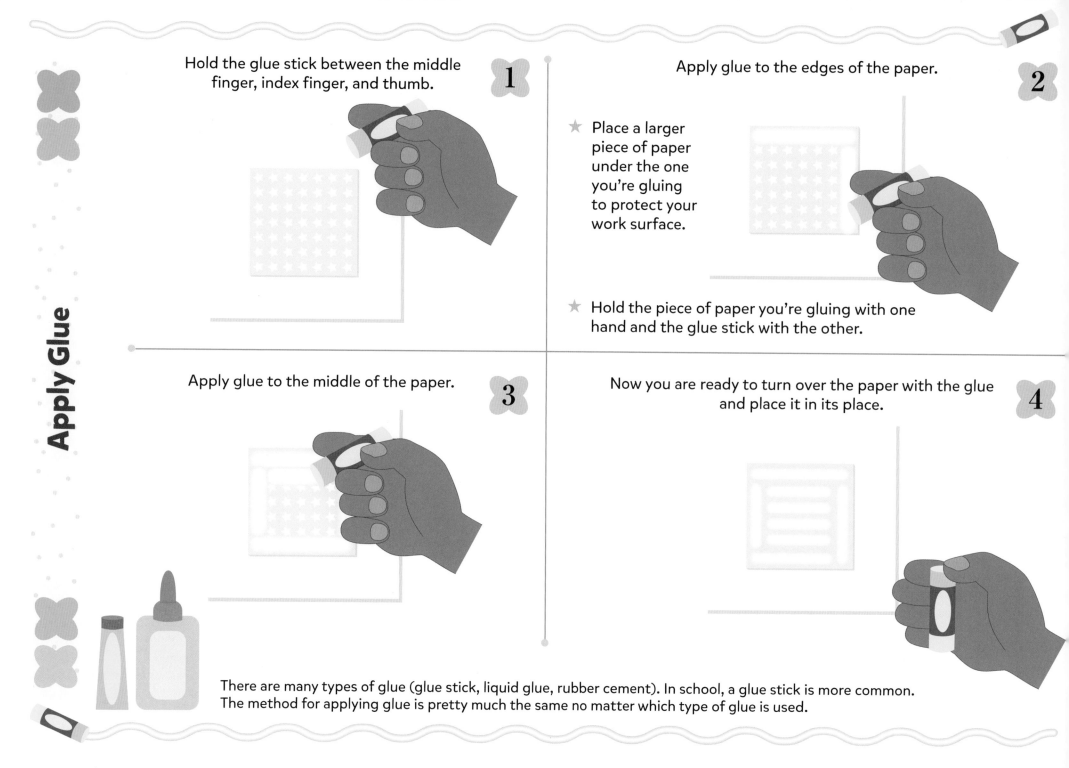

1 Hold the glue stick between the middle finger, index finger, and thumb.

2 Apply glue to the edges of the paper.

★ Place a larger piece of paper under the one you're gluing to protect your work surface.

★ Hold the piece of paper you're gluing with one hand and the glue stick with the other.

3 Apply glue to the middle of the paper.

4 Now you are ready to turn over the paper with the glue and place it in its place.

There are many types of glue (glue stick, liquid glue, rubber cement). In school, a glue stick is more common. The method for applying glue is pretty much the same no matter which type of glue is used.

Cut Hair

To Parents: In this activity, cut the gray lines and have your child cut the boy's hair any way they like. This freestyle cut gives them practice cutting in a straight line with scissors. If this seems difficult, show them how to do it first.

Parents — Cut the gray lines.

How to Play

Cut the boy's hair any way you like.

Complete

Cut the gray lines.

Sticker

★Good job!★

Make Fireworks

To Parents: This activity focuses on cutting short straight lines. Any pattern is okay for gluing, as long as the pieces are placed within the blue circle.

Parents

Cut the gray lines.

• How to Play •

1 Cut each strip into smaller pieces.

2 Cover the blue circle with glue.

3 Place the cut pieces anywhere you like.

Complete

When the glue dries, the activity is complete.

Cut the gray lines.

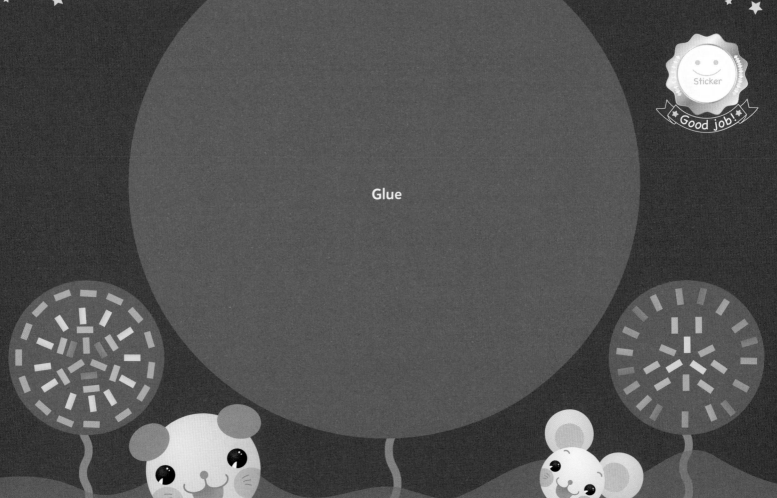

Glue

Sticker

Good job!

Use for page 6.

Use for this page.

Fill the Field with Flowers

To Parents: In this activity, your child will practice cutting short lines as shown on the previous page. After they're done, praise your child, saying, "The animals look happy among the flowers."

Parents

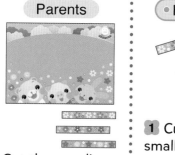

Cut the gray lines.

• How to Play •

1 Cut each strip into smaller pieces without cutting the flowers.

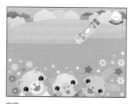

2 Cover the green area of the field with glue.

3 Place the cut pieces anywhere you like.

Complete

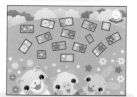

When the glue dries, the activity is complete.

Glue

Glue

Sticker

Good job!

Use for page 5.

Use for this page.

Decorate the Cake

To Parents: Have your child practice cutting short lines. Your child should keep the scissors open and close them only slightly to make the cuts at the base of the scissors, without closing the scissors all the way.

Parents

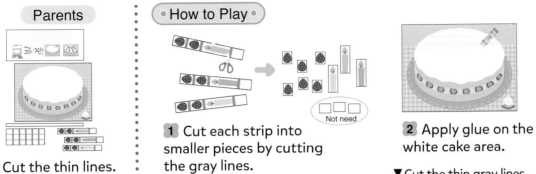

Cut the thin lines.

• How to Play •

1 Cut each strip into smaller pieces by cutting the gray lines.

Not need

2 Apply glue on the white cake area.

▼ Cut the thin gray lines.

Complete

3 Place the cut pieces of strawberries and candles anywhere you like.

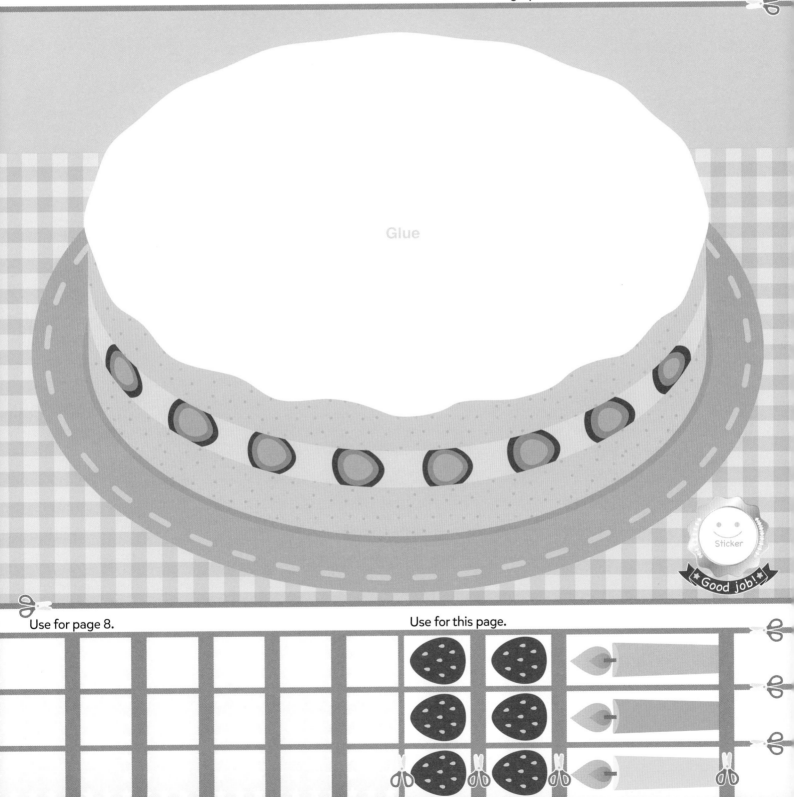

Glue

Sticker

★Good job!★

Use for page 8.

Use for this page.

Line Up Ants

To Parents: After your child cuts out the pieces, place the pieces on the page before gluing them in place. Uneven distances between ants are no problem. After the ants are lined up, say to your child, "You lined up a lot of ants!"

Parents

Cut the thin lines.

• How to Play •

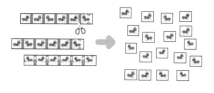

1 Cut each strip into smaller pieces by cutting the gray lines.

2 Cover the path to the chocolate with glue.

Complete

3 Place the ants so that they look as if they are marching to the chocolate.

Glue

Sticker

★ Good job! ★

Chocolate

Use for page 7.

Use for this page.

Make Sunshine

To Parents: In this activity, your child will practice cutting straight lines partway through. Have your child make small cuts only at the base of the scissors. It's not necessary for the number and length of the cuts to be the same as those in the sample.

Parents

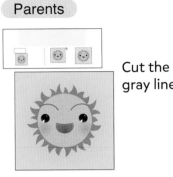

Cut the gray line.

• How to Play •

Make cuts in the yellow area to make sunshine.

Complete

Cut the gray line.

Drive through Town

To Parents: Have your child cut the lines on both sides of each building. Then fold the sides to stand them up. Because it is difficult to fold part of the way, show your child how to fold so part of the paper remains standing.

Parents

Cut the thin lines.

How to Make • Learn how to play on page 12.

1 Cut the thick gray lines.

2 Fold along the —·— and stand the buildings and houses up.

Fold

Fold

Cut the thin, gray lines.

Cut the thin, gray lines.

Parking

Parking

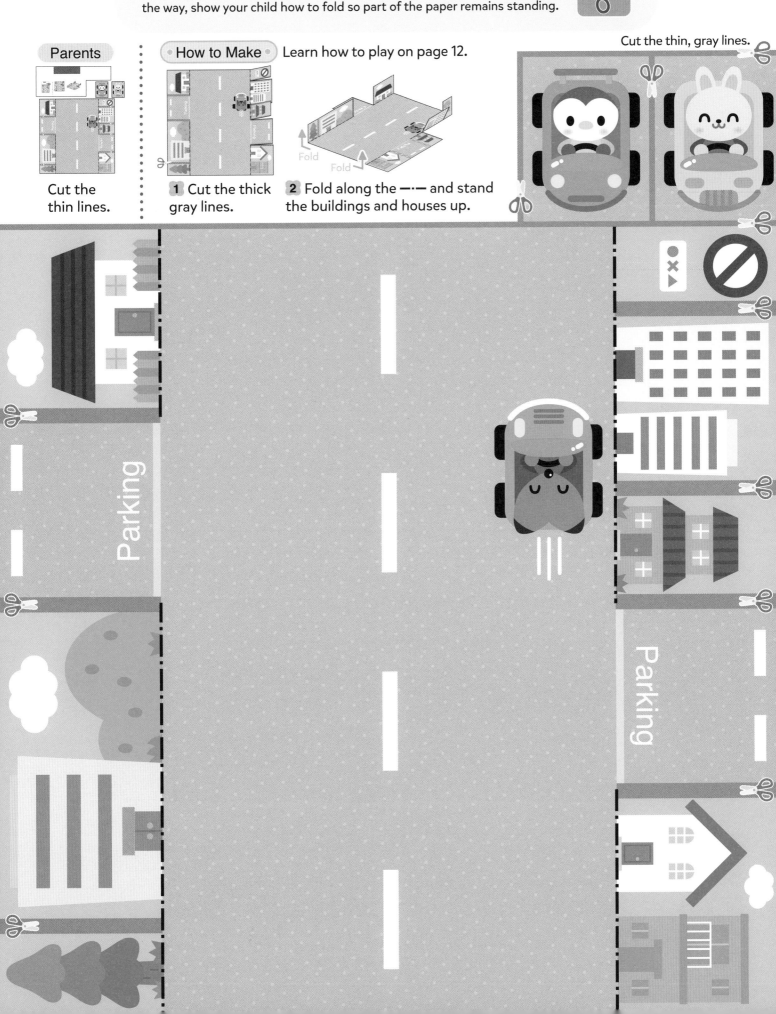

Complete

How to Play

Drive the cars through the town!

Good job!

Sticker

Make an Octopus

To Parents: Have your child cut the thick lines until they stop. After your child successfully cuts only at the base of the scissors, practice cutting while moving the paper, not the position of the scissors. Show your child first how to cut while moving the paper.

Parents Cut the thin line.

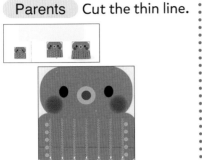

How to Make

Learn how to play on page 14.

Cut the thick gray lines.

Complete

Cut this line first.

How to Play

Shake the octopus
to make it dance!

Sticker

Good job!

Make Fruits

To Parents: After your child successfully cuts only at the base of the scissors, have them practice cutting while moving the paper, not the position of the scissors. This requires your child to make longer cuts and gives them more advanced practice in stopping when cutting.

Parents

Cut the thin gray line.

• How to Play •

1 Cut the thick gray line.

2 Put the pieces together to make a pumpkin.

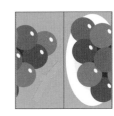

3 Turn over the pieces and put them together to make grapes.

Cut this line first.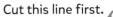

Sticker

Good job!

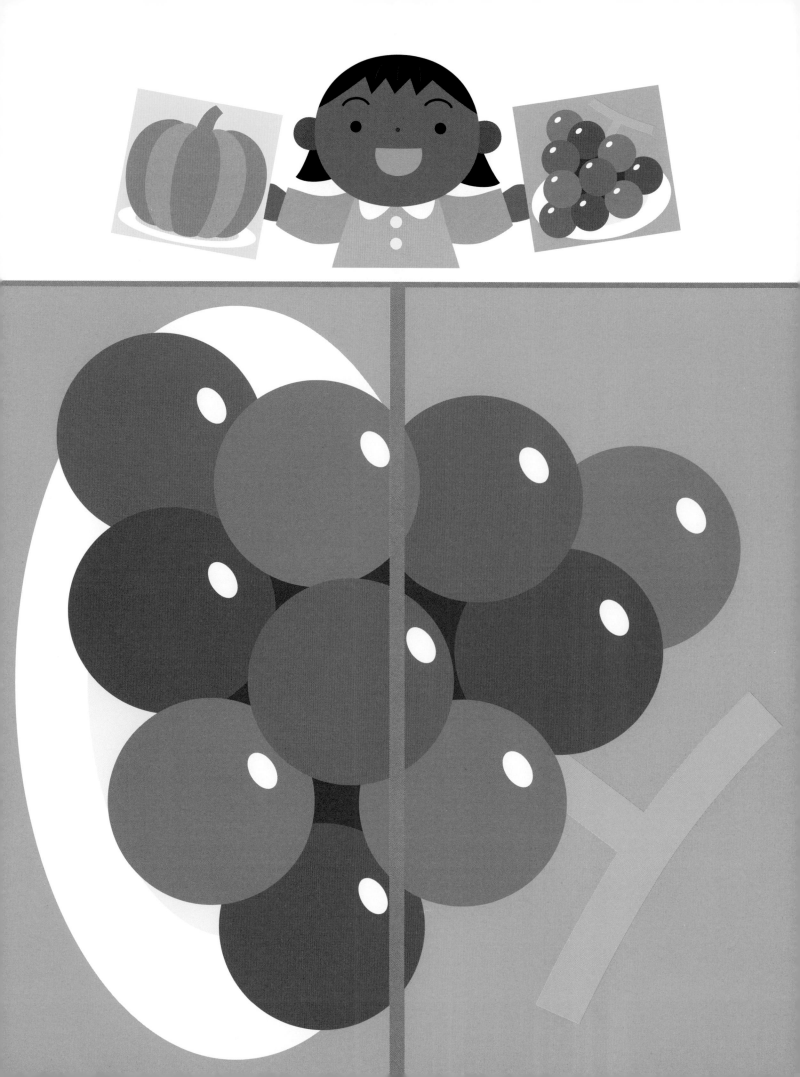

Make a Bird and a Fish

To Parents: On this page, have your child put the pieces together, beginning by aligning the positions of the eye and the head. If this seems difficult for your child, use the image of the bird on page 18 as a reference.

Parents

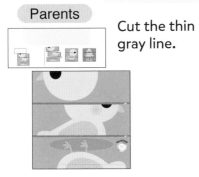

Cut the thin gray line.

▼ Cut this line first.

• How to Play •

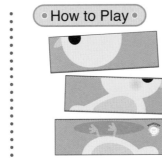

1 Cut the thick gray lines.

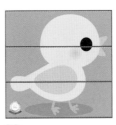

2 Put the pieces together to make a bird.

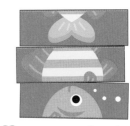

3 Turn over the pieces and put them together to make a fish.

Good Job!

Sticker

Make Trains ①

To Parents: For the remaining activities, your child should cut all the lines on their own. Have your child connect the train compartments while paying attention to the shapes and colors of the train.

How to Make
Use this page and page 21 to make the trains.
Learn how to play on page 20.

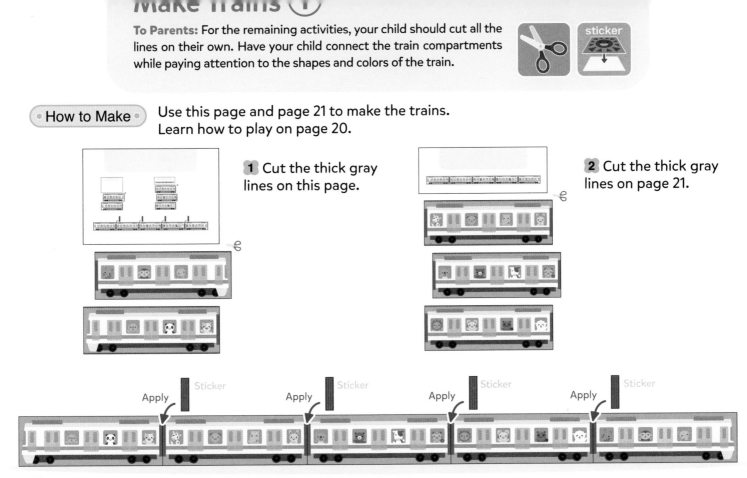

1 Cut the thick gray lines on this page.

2 Cut the thick gray lines on page 21.

Apply   Sticker   Apply   Sticker   Apply   Sticker   Apply   Sticker

3 Apply the stickers to connect the train compartments.

Cut this line first.

Sticker

Sticker

Make the trains move!

Subway train

Locomotive train

Make Trains 2

To Parents: The pictures of the beginning and end pieces are fixed, but the three in the middle can be arranged in any order.

See page 19 for directions. Learn how to play on page 20.

Complete

Cut this line first.

Sticker

Make a Crab 1

To Parents: This activity allows your child to practice gluing pieces to a specific location. Make sure your child gives the crab four legs on each side. Have scrap paper under the crab while your child glues on its legs.

How to Make Use this page and page 25 to make the crab. See page 24 for a completed crab and learn how to play on page 25.

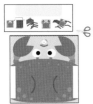 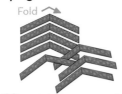  

1 Cut the thick gray lines on this page and page 25.

2 Fold along each — — — to bend the crab's legs.

3 Apply glue to the white areas on the sides of the crab's body.

4 Glue the legs to the crab.

Good job!

Sticker

Glue

Glue

Complete

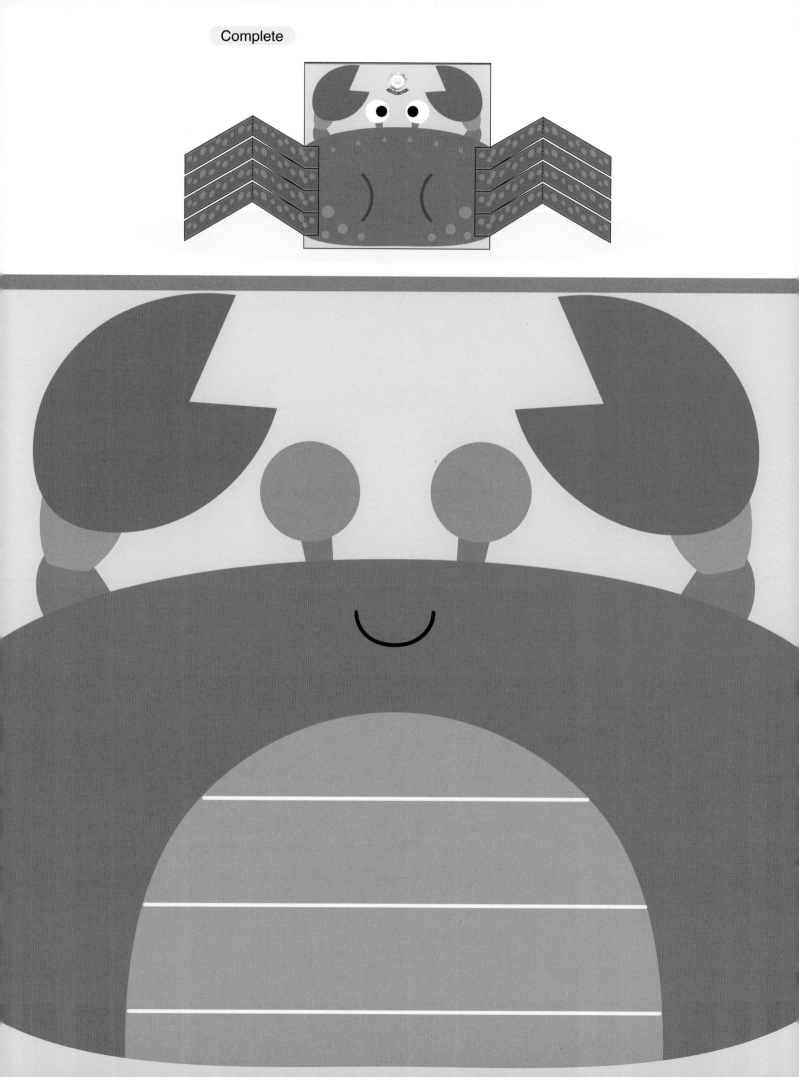

Make a Crab ②

To Parents: After gluing on its legs, have your child shake the crab to make it walk!

(• How to Play •)   Use this page and page 23 to make the crab. Shake the crab to make it walk!

Cut this line first.

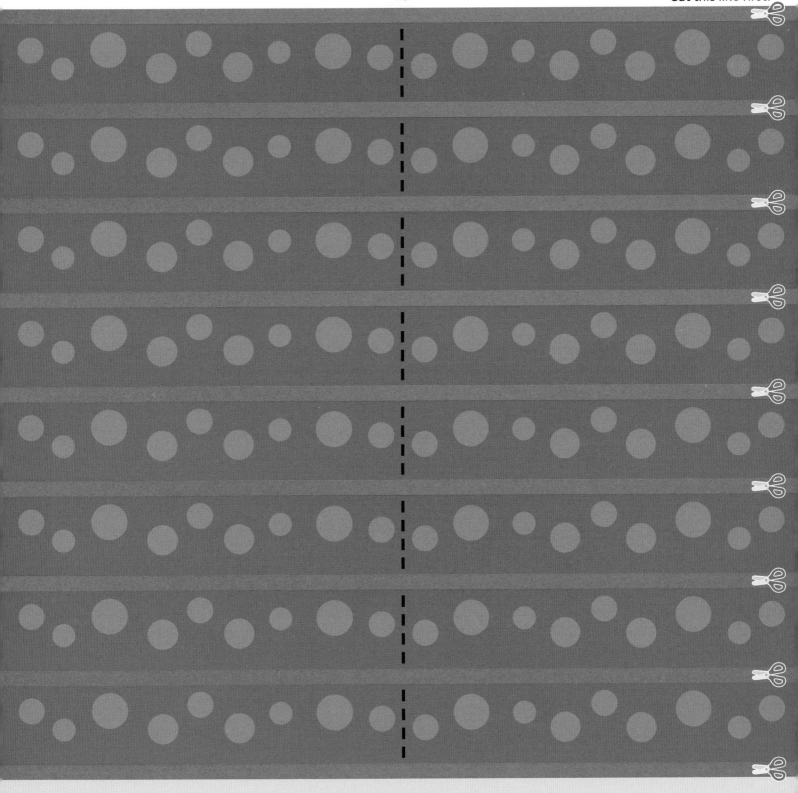

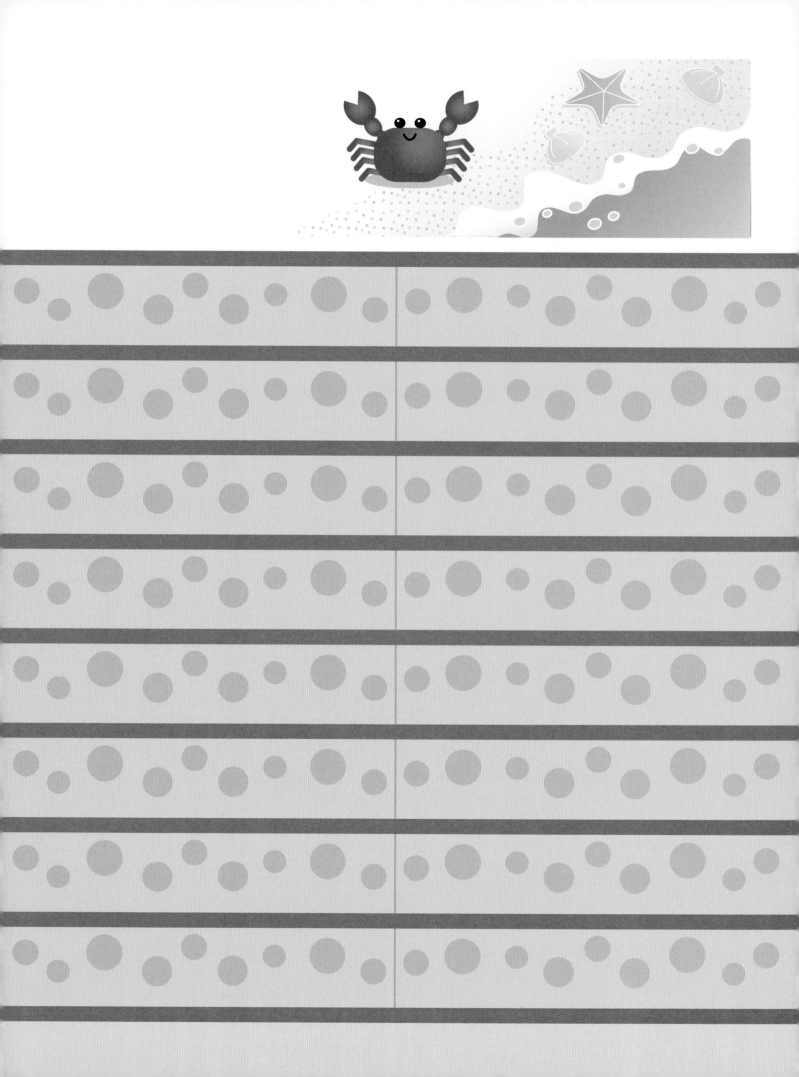

Stack Animals

To Parents: This activity asks your child to fold paper and stand it up. After cutting the paper, have your child fold it in the middle so it stands up. They can try to find the best way to make it stand by changing how wide the paper is open.

How to Make   Learn how to play on page 28.

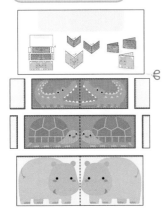

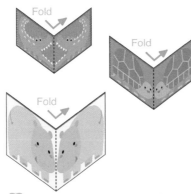

Complete

1 Cut the thick gray lines.

2 Fold each animal and make it stand up.

Cut this line first.

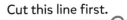

Stack the animals on top of one another!

Make a Fire Truck

To Parents: The remaining activities become more complex. Assist your child through the steps of each activity. For this activity, fold the paper in half so it can stand up. Then put the ladder on top and move it move it up and down!

How to Make Learn how to play on page 30.

1 Cut the thick gray lines.

2 Fold the truck and make it stand up.

Place it on top.

3 Fold the ladder and place it on top of the truck.

Fold

Complete

Cut this line first.

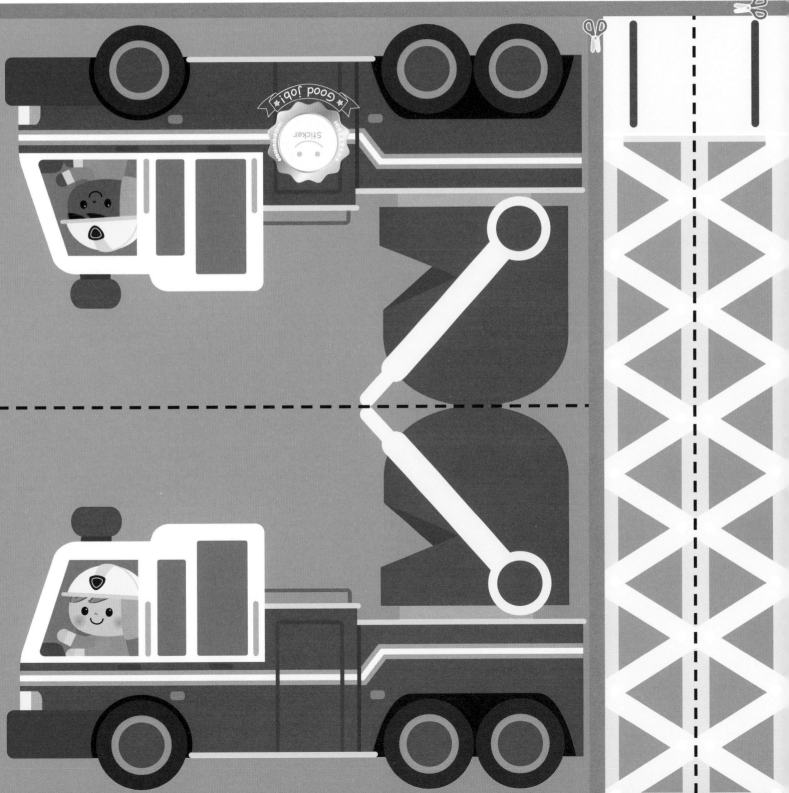

Raise the ladder like it would
on a real fire truck!

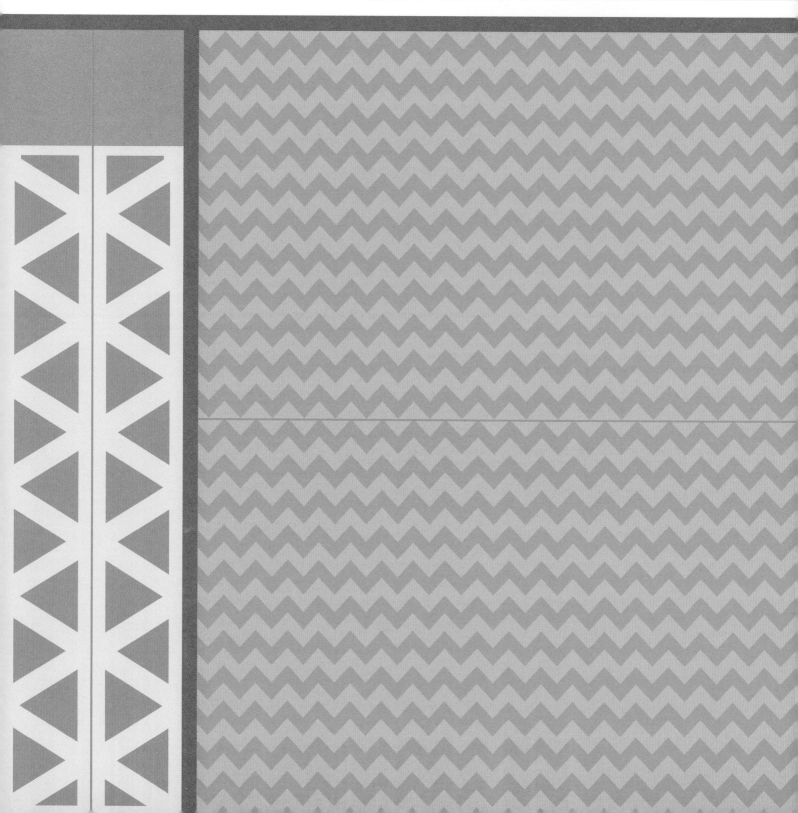

To Parents: Ask your child to first cut out the animals. By using the base of the scissors, your child can then clean up the edges and make them as straight as possible.

How to Make Use this page to make the wrestlers. See page 33 for a completed picture, and learn how to play on page 32.

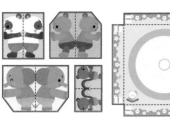  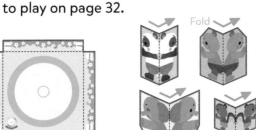

1 Cut the thick gray lines.

2 Fold each animal and make it stand.

3 Fold the edges and apply the stickers to make a ring.

Fold

Apply sticker

Apply sticker

Cut this line first.

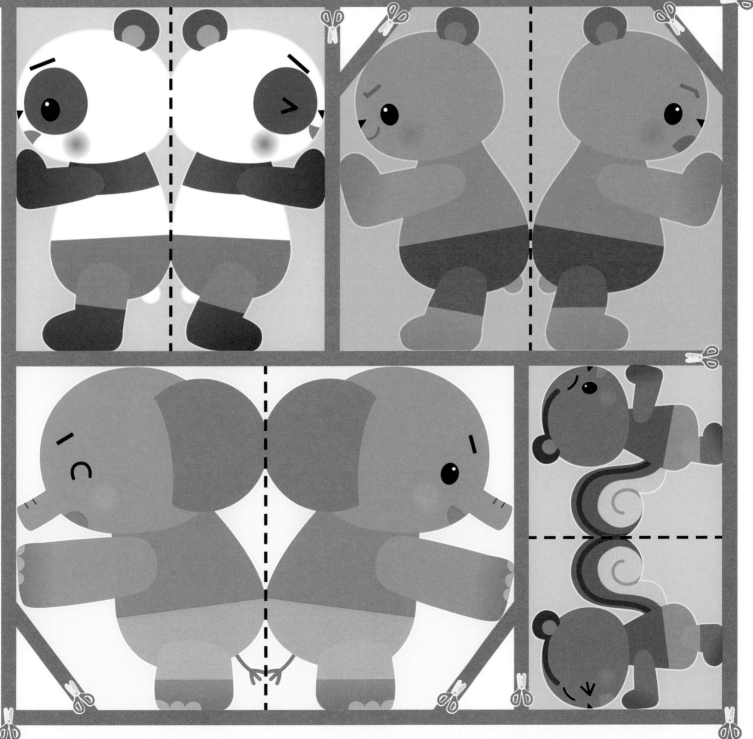

child's animal fall out of the ring or fall down. The remaining standing animal is the winner!

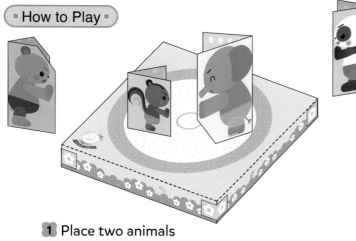

How to Play

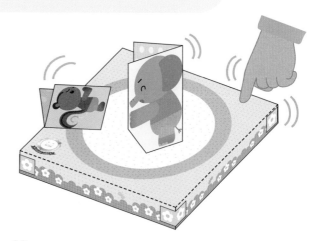

1 Place two animals face-to-face in the ring.

2 Tap the ring to make the opponent fall out of the ring or fall down.

To Parents: Make sure your child cuts the line across the page first and then trims the pieces. Encourage your child to cut the corners carefully. If this is difficult, make creases before they start cutting.

Use this page to make the ring. Learn how to play on pages 32 and 34.

Complete

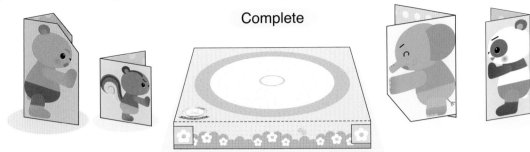

Cut this line first.

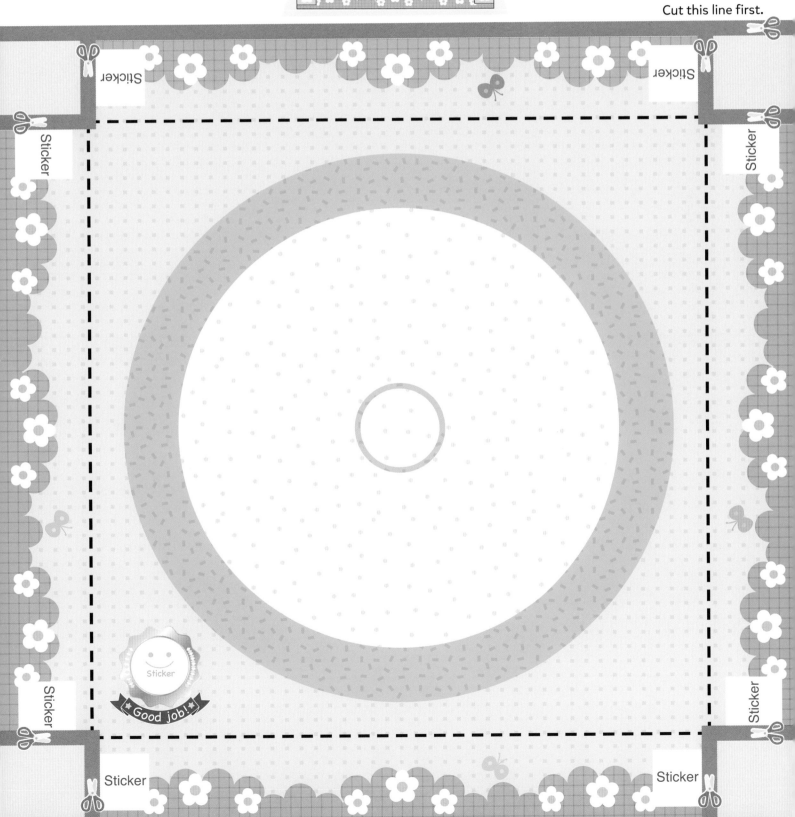

Sticker

Sticker

Sticker

Sticker

Sticker

Sticker

Sticker

Sticker

Good job.

Sticker

Sticker

the one who knocks their opponent to the ground or pushes them out of the ring.

Make a Polar Bear Slide

To Parents: If this activity seems difficult for your child, help them by making slight creases. If the penguins do not slide easily, try adjusting the angle of their bottom folds.

How to Make Learn how to play on page 36.

1 Cut the thick gray lines.

2 Fold the slide and make it stand up.

3 Fold the penguins and place them on the slide.

Fold

Fold

Fold

Fold

Fold

Complete

Cut this line first.

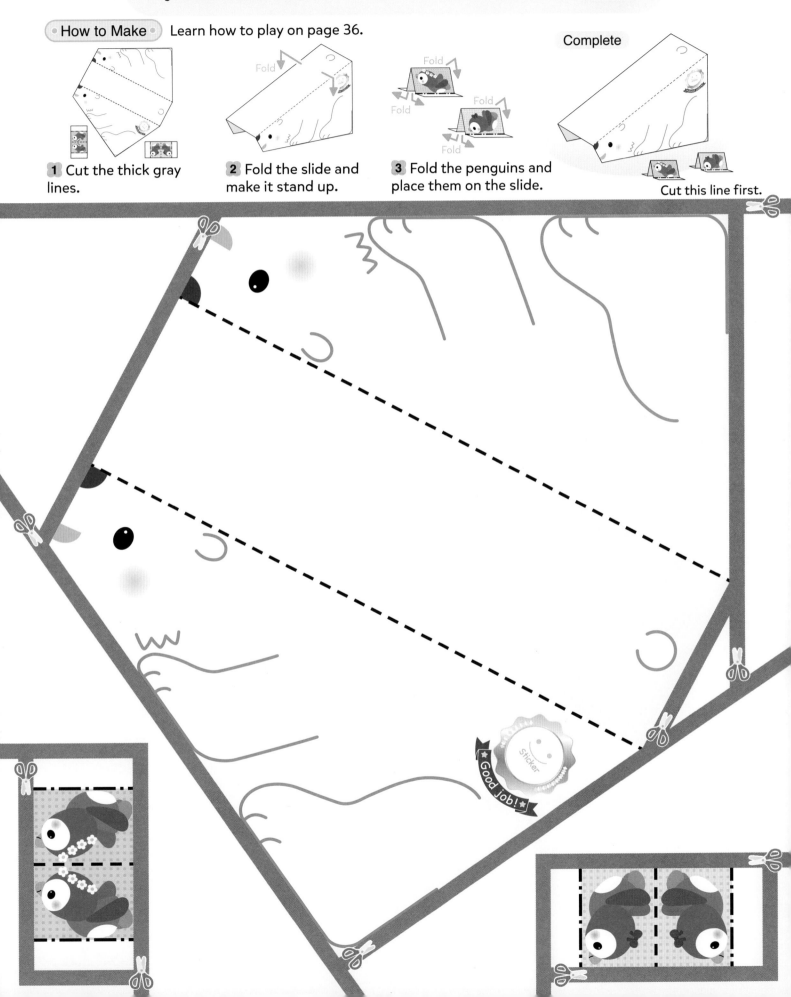

Place the penguins on top of the polar bear slide. Then let them slide down!

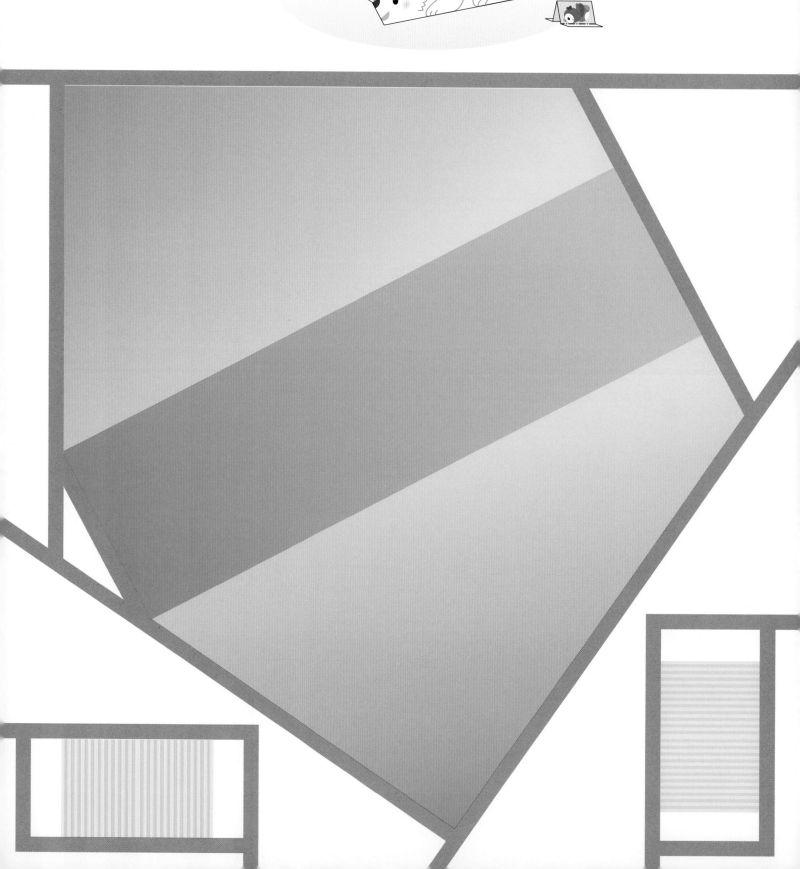

See What Appears

To Parents: This activity allows your child to practice making an accordion fold. When they're done folding and unfolding, ask your child what comes out of the box.

How to Make Learn how to play on page 38.

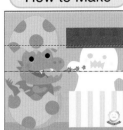 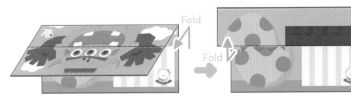

Fold

Fold

Complete

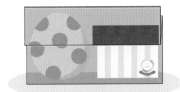

1 Cut the thick gray line. **2** Fold in and out to make an accordion fold.

Cut this line first.

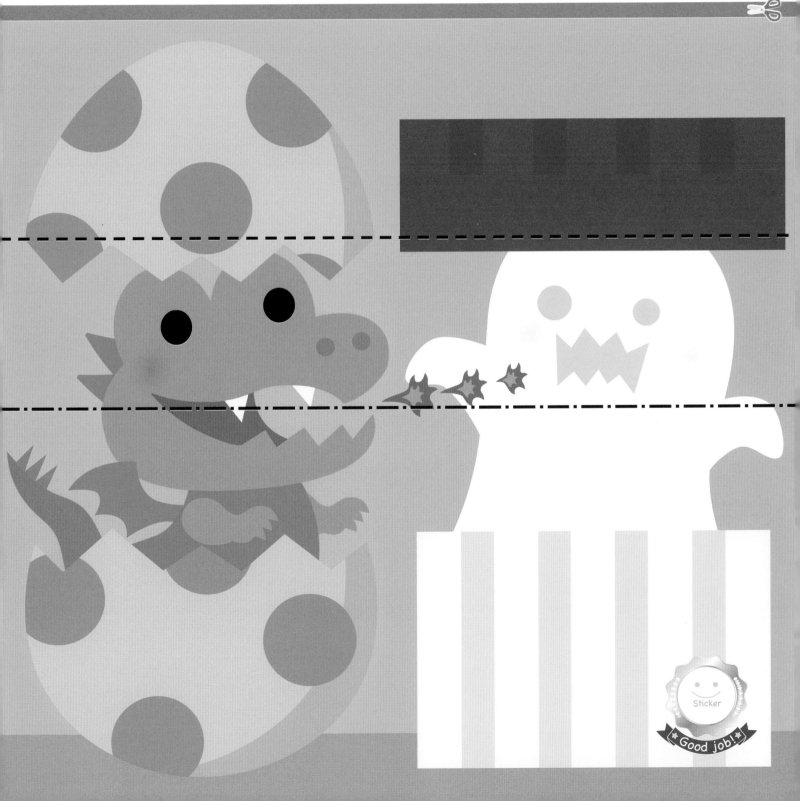

Sticker

Good job!

• How to Play •

Pull upward to find out what
will hatch from the egg and
what's inside the box.

Roar!

Boo!

Flip the page over and
pull upward to see
what's hiding in the hill.

Make a Strong Gorilla

To Parents: In this activity, your child will practice cutting halfway through the paper. Make sure your child folds the paper in half before cutting the center line.

How to Make   Learn how to play on page 40.

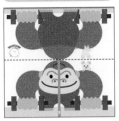

1 Cut the horizontal thick gray line.

2 Fold the piece in half.

3 Cut the vertical thick gray line.

Complete

Cut this line first.

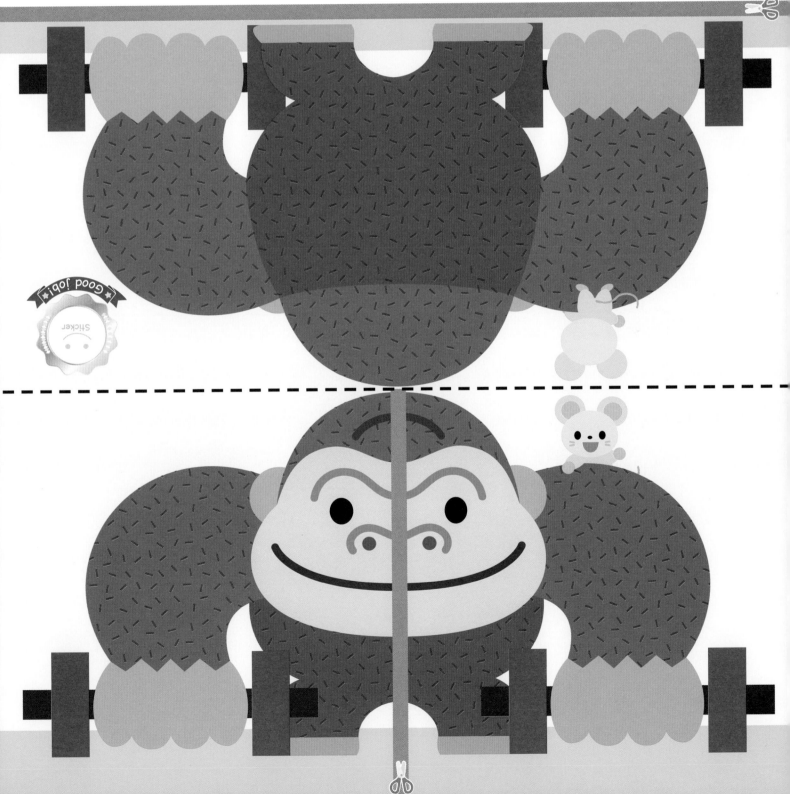

Good Job!

Sticker

How to Play

Lift one arm at a time to
make the gorilla exercise!

Fill the Refrigerator

To Parents: Make sure your child first cuts the refrigerator from the page. Then they can cut the refrigerator doors and food pieces. Ask your child to tell you what is in the refrigerator.

• How to Make • Learn how to play on page 42.

1 Cut the thick gray lines.

2 Fold in the pieces.

Fold   Fold

Complete

Cut the gray lines.

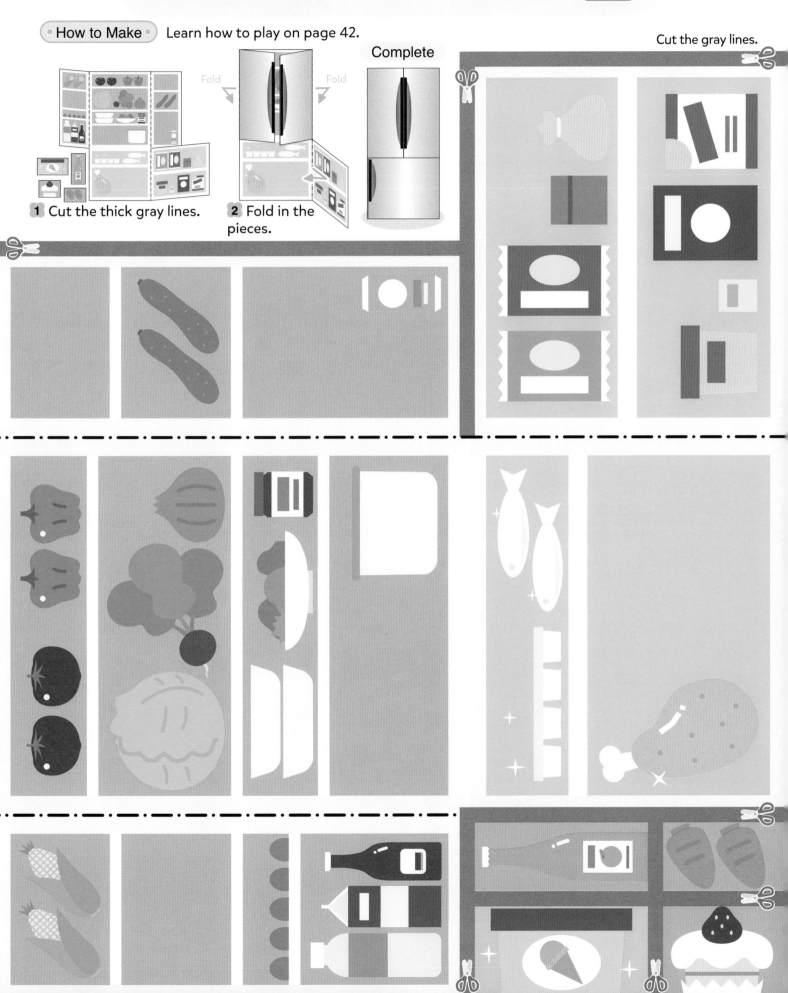

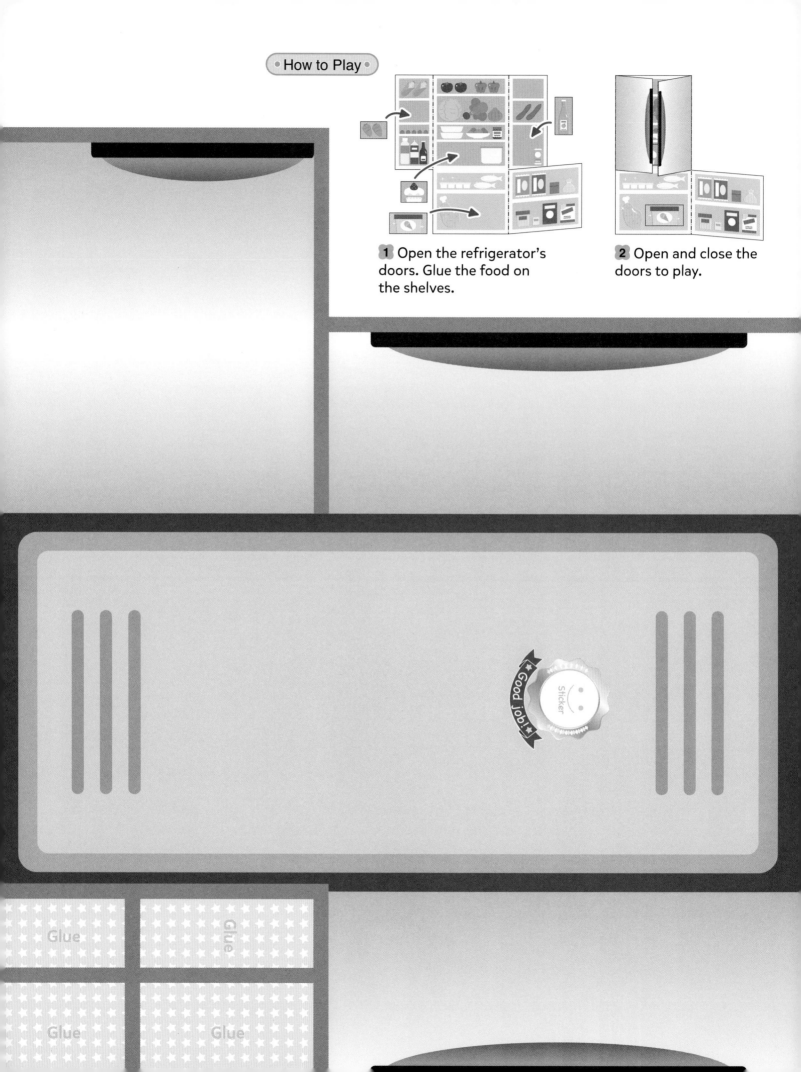

1 Open the refrigerator's doors. Glue the food on the shelves.

2 Open and close the doors to play.

Good job!

Sticker

Glue

Glue

Glue

Glue

Ninja Surprise!

To Parents: In this activity, your child will practice cutting right angles. When they cut to a corner, have them turn the paper. If this is difficult, they can cut to the corner from both ends. The goal is to stop cutting partway through the paper.

(How to Make) Learn how to play on page 44.

Complete

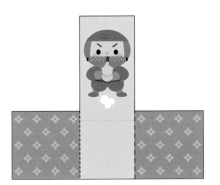

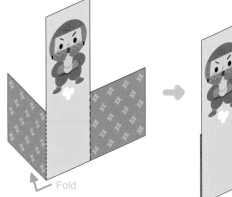

Fold

Fold

Ninja surprise!

1 Cut the thick gray lines.

2 Fold the pieces as shown.

Cut this line first.

How to Play

Pull the flaps to the side to find out what the ninja changes into.

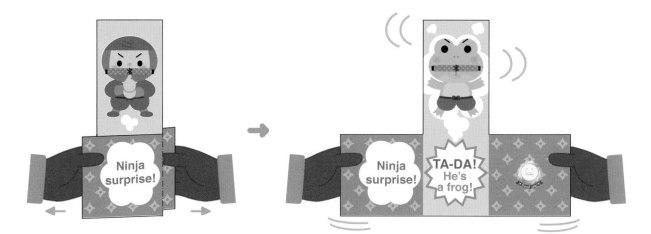

Play Ring Toss

To Parents: Have your child cut the long lines by making short cuts only at the base of the scissors. Show your child how to apply glue, roll the strip of paper, and attach the ends to make a ring. Then let them try.

How to Make Learn how to play on page 46.

1 Cut the thick gray lines.

Fold

2 Fold the seal to make it stand.

Roll it

Glue it

Apply sticker

Roll it

Glue it

Apply sticker

Complete

3 Roll each strip and glue the edges together to make a ring. Then place a sticker on each white box.

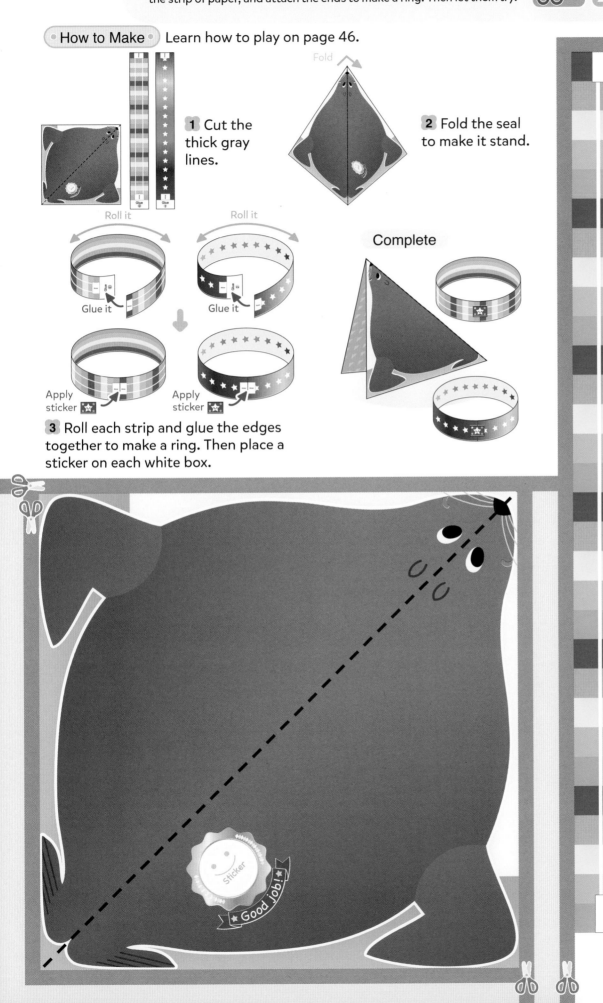

Sticker

Sticker

Sticker

Sticker

Sticker

Glue
1

Glue
2

Good job!

sticker

How to Play

Toss a ring through the seal's nose!

To Parents: This activity allows your child to practice making an accordion fold. Make the creases for your child at first. Then have them try folding.

(How to Make) Learn how to play on page 48.

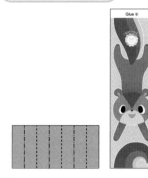

1 Cut the thick gray lines.

Roll it

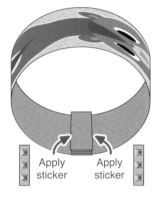

Glue it

2 Roll the squirrel strip and glue the edges together to make a ring.

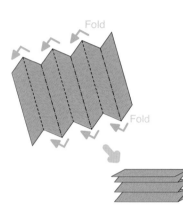

Fold

Fold

3 Fold the green strip in and out to make an accordion fold.

Apply sticker   Apply sticker

4 Put the folded green strip inside the squirrel roll and apply the stickers as shown.

Complete

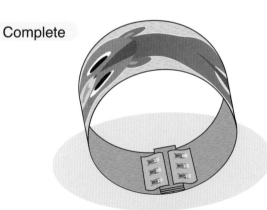

Glue **I**

Good job!

Sticker

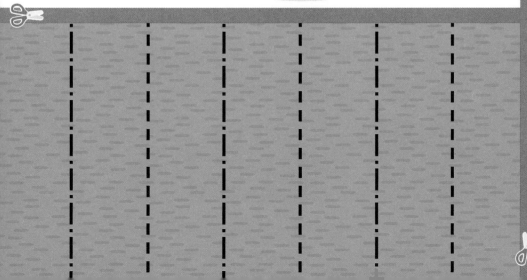

Place the folded green strip here.

Roll the squirrel and watch it wobble!

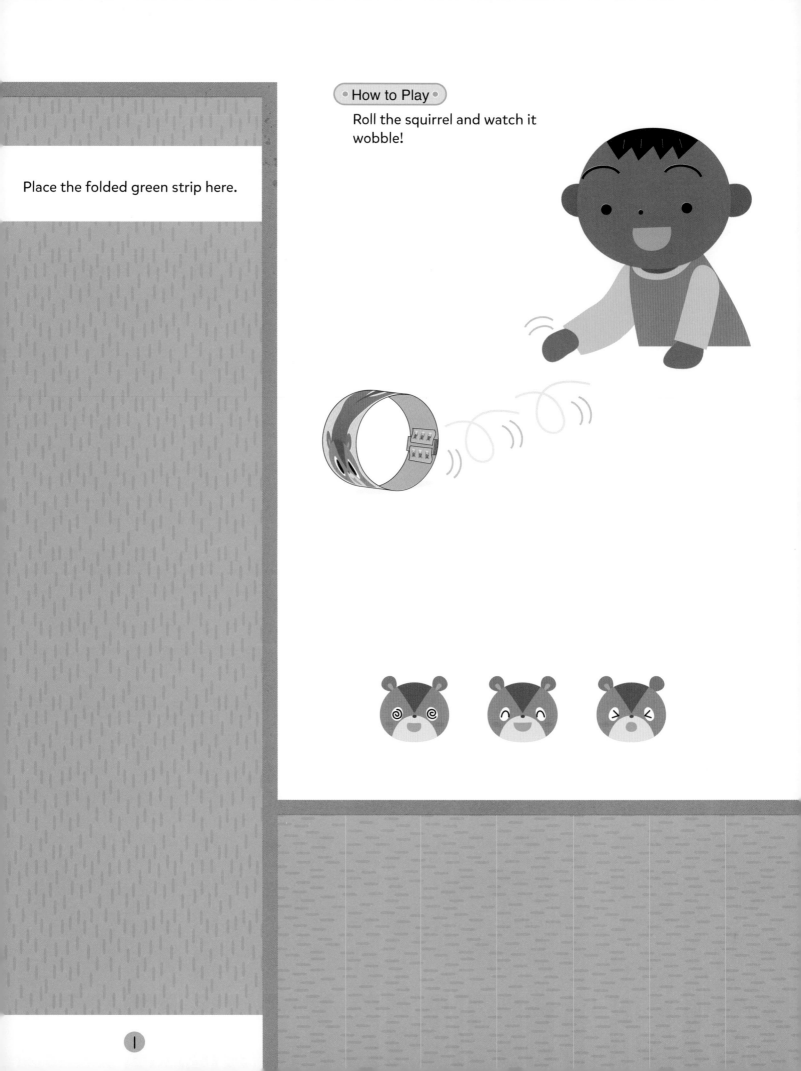

To Parents: In this activity, your child will cut lines of different lengths. Start with the short lines. If your child can cut the long lines, praise them by saying, "Well done!" Your child may need help gluing a ring over other ring, as this can be difficult.

How to Make Learn how to play on page 50.

1 Cut the thick gray lines.

Roll it — Glue it

2 Roll each strip and glue the edges together to make a ring.

See page 50 for more directions.

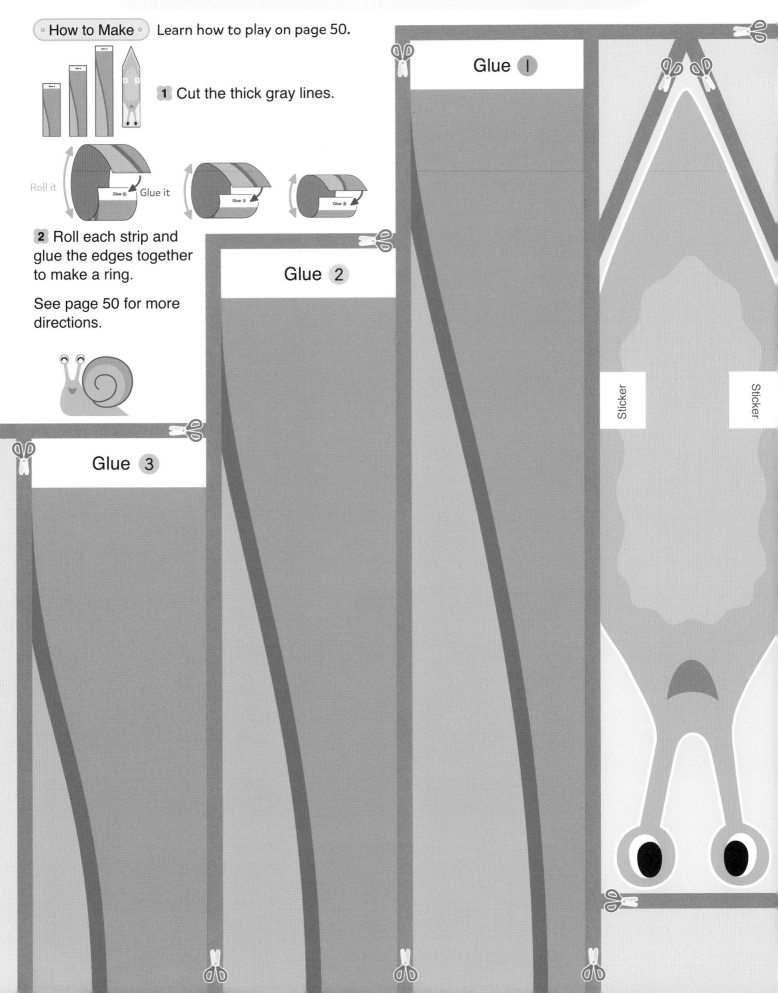

Glue 1

Glue 2

Glue 3

Sticker

Sticker

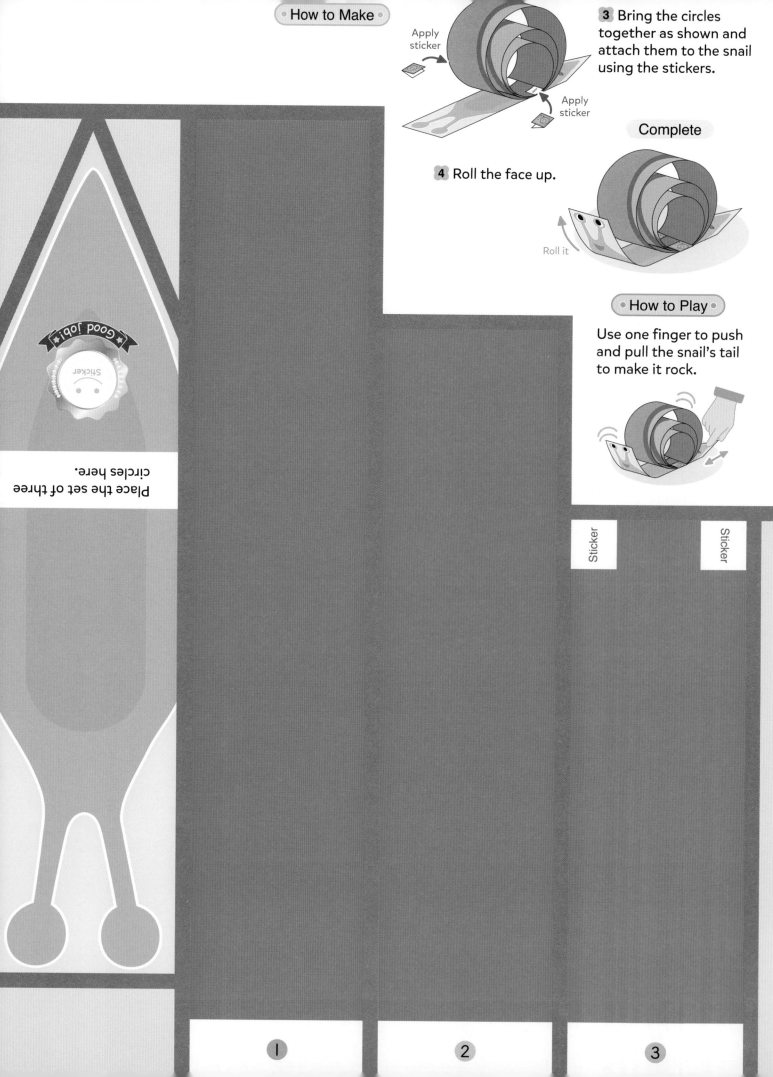

How to Make

Apply sticker

3 Bring the circles together as shown and attach them to the snail using the stickers.

Apply sticker

4 Roll the face up.

Complete

Roll it

How to Play

Use one finger to push and pull the snail's tail to make it rock.

Good job!

Sticker

Place the set of three circles here.

Sticker

Sticker

How to Make

1

2

3

Make a Caterpillar

To Parents: Have your child connect the rings by inserting a strip inside one ring. As it may be difficult to glue both ends of the ring, hold it steady for your child. When they are able to do it, use more paper to make party decorations.

How to Make Learn how to play on page 52.

1 Cut the thick gray lines.

Glue it · Roll it · Roll it · Glue it · Glue it · Roll it · Roll it · Glue it · Glue it

2 Roll a strip and glue its edges together to make a ring. Then insert another strip inside the first. Then roll and glue it together. Repeat until all the strips are connected.

Apply sticker

Complete

3 Attach the caterpillar's face to a ring using the stickers.

Sticker

Glue 1

Glue 2

Glue 3

Sticker

Glue 4

How to Play

Pull the caterpillar's face to make it walk!

Sticker

Sticker

1

2

3

4

Make Puzzle Boxes

To Parents: The next few activities allow your child to practice making cubes. To make a cube, crease and assemble before gluing the ends together. This helps your child with forward thinking and planning ahead.

How to Make Learn how to play on page 54.

1 Cut the thick gray lines.

2 Fold each strip along – – – and glue the edges together.

Complete

Makes 4 cubes total.

Glue 1

Glue 2

Glue 3

Glue 4

Line up the boxes and
match their colors!

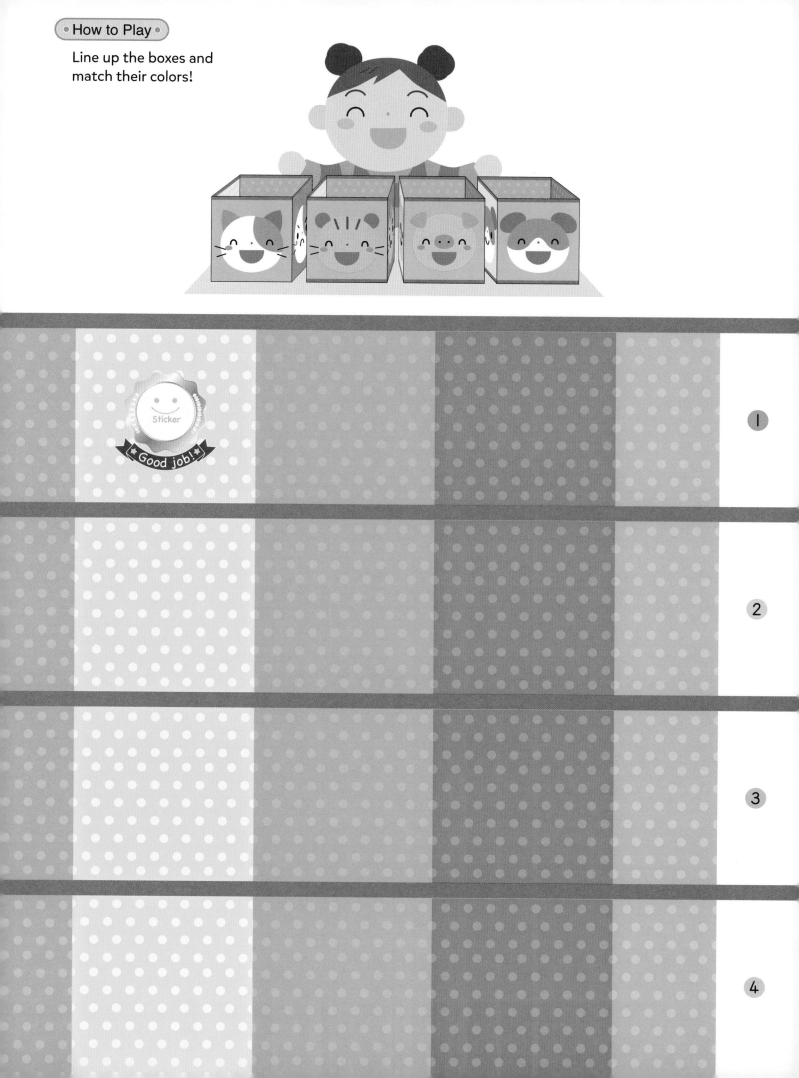

Sticker
★ Good job! ★

1

2

3

4

Make a Cable Car

To Parents: This activity uses two separate pieces to make one box. Make creases to assemble before gluing the ends together. Your child can help confirm the places to glue.

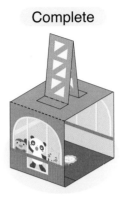

String or Thread

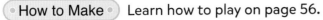

How to Make Learn how to play on page 56.

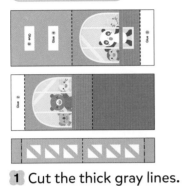

1 Cut the thick gray lines.

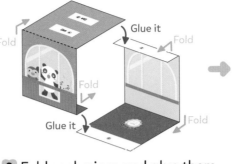

Fold
Glue it
Fold
Fold
Glue it
Fold

2 Fold each piece and glue them together by matching the numbers.

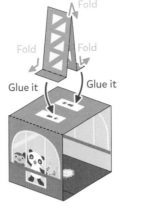

Fold
Fold
Fold
Glue it
Glue it

Complete

Glue 3

Glue 4

Glue 1

Glue 2

• How to Play •

1 Thread the string through the cable car as in the picture.

2 Let the cable car slide!

...child... Cut a piece of string or thread. Hold one end while your child holds the other so you can play together.

Make a Snake

To Parents: This activity allows your child to practice making an accordion fold. Make slight creases before your child folds the paper.

How to Make   Learn how to play on page 58.

1 Cut the thick gray lines.

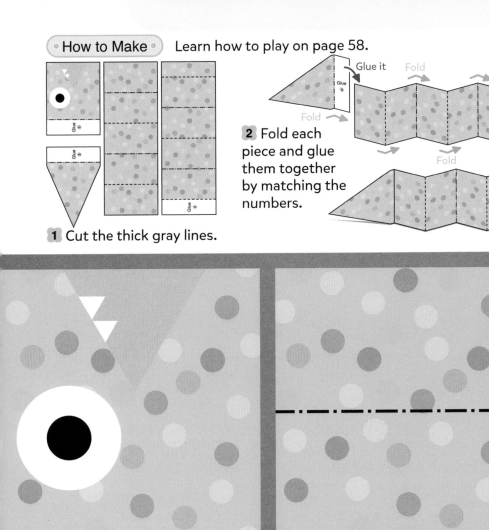

2 Fold each piece and glue them together by matching the numbers.

Complete

Glue **1**

Glue **3**

Glue **2**

Shake the snake back and forth to see it move!

Help the snake slither along on the ground.

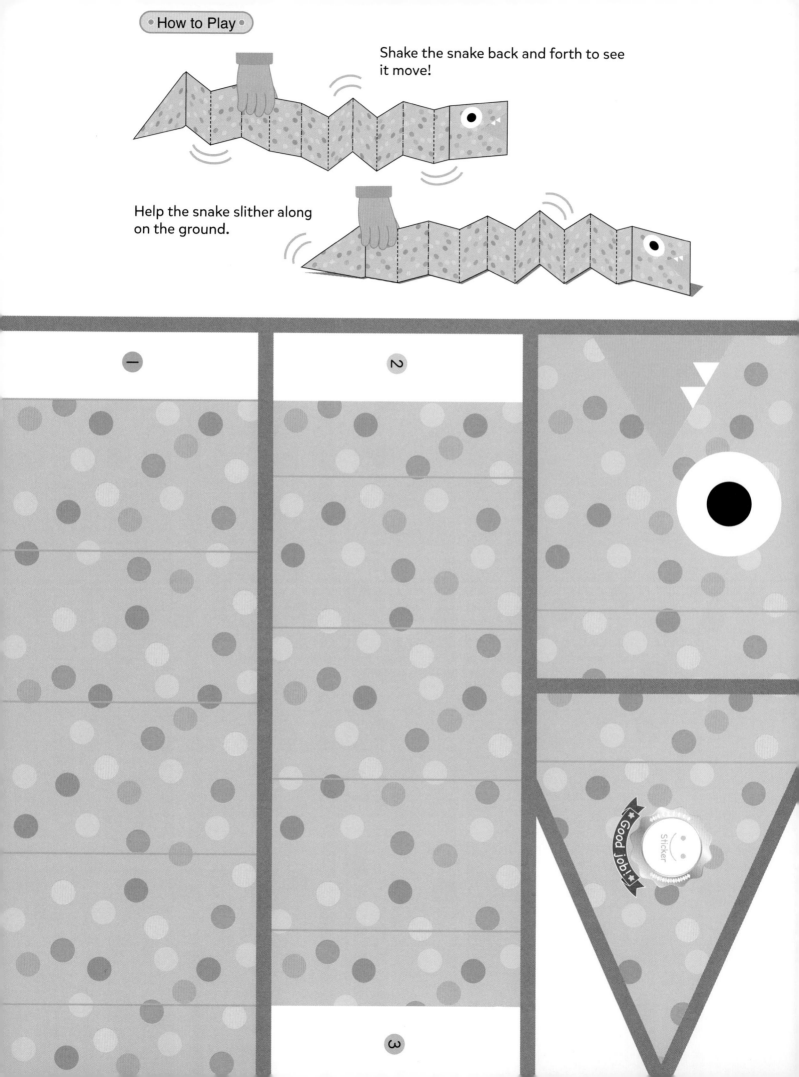

1

2

3

Sticker

Good job!

Make Jumping Animals

To Parents: If your child needs help, start by making slight creases. Show that animals jump differently depending on how the paper is folded.

• How to Make • Learn how to play on page 60.

1 Cut the thick gray lines.

Complete

2 Fold each animal's legs and glue its body and head together.

Glue it

Fold Fold Fold Fold Fold

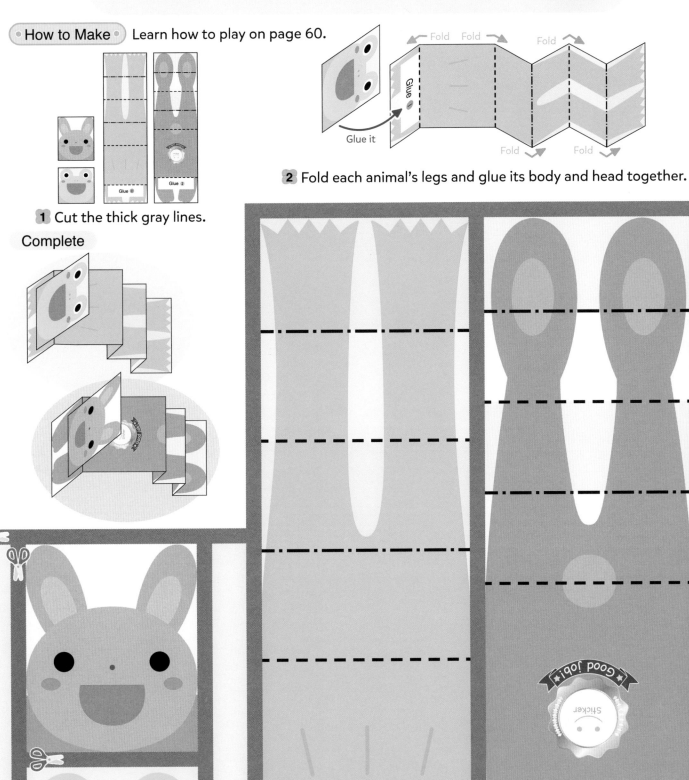

Glue 1

Glue 2

Good job!

Sticker

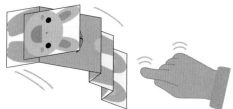

1 Press down lightly with your finger.

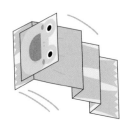

2 Slide your finger slowly off the paper to make the rabbit jump!

Play with the frog in the same way.

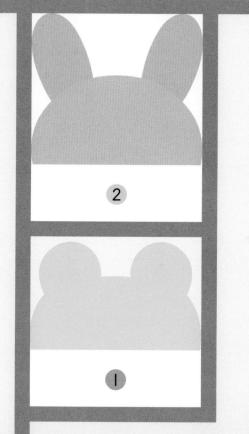

Make a Mask

To Parents: Before gluing, have your child make sure the numbers are in the correct place. It may be difficult for your child to attach the rubber band, so your assistance may be needed.

• How to Make • Learn how to play on page 62.

1 Cut the thick gray lines.

2 Fold the dog's head and glue its ears in place.

Glue

Fold

3 Glue the paper strips to the back of the dog's head.

Fold　　　Glue

4 Attach a rubber band using the stickers on either side to hold the strips together.

Place sticker　　Rubber band

Roll it

Rubber band

sticker

glue

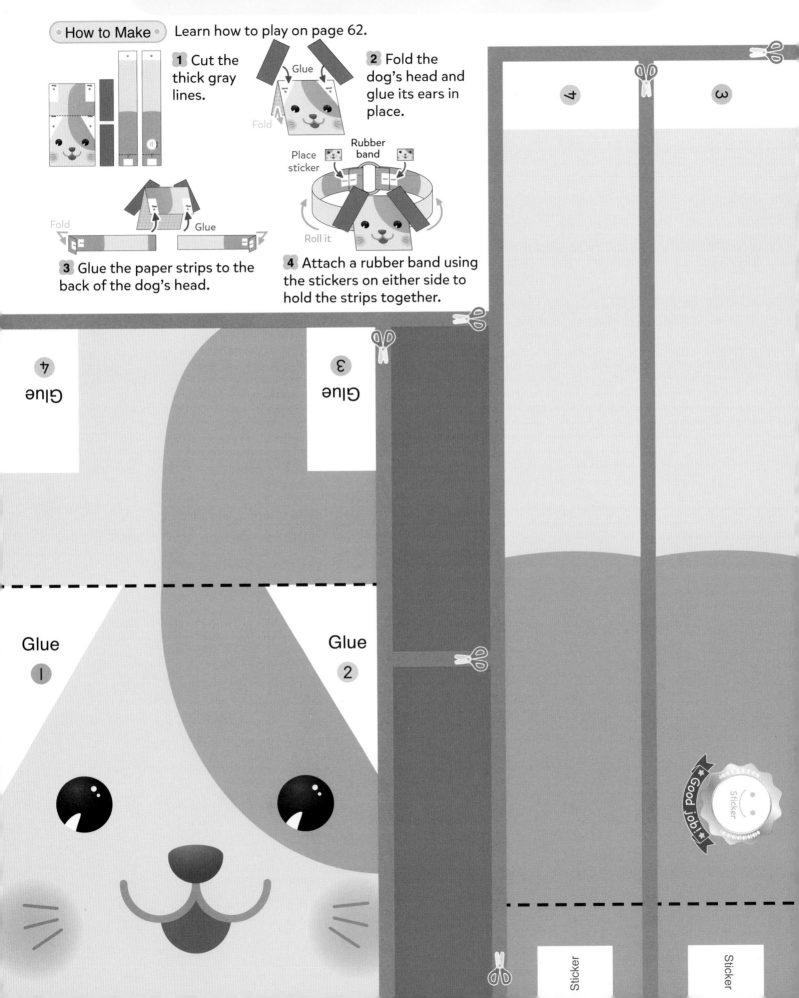

4 Glue

3 Glue

Glue
I

Glue
2

Good job!
Sticker

Sticker

Sticker

Complete

How to Play

Put the mask on and pretend to be a dog!

2

1

Sticker

Sticker

To Parents: Fold the paper once to make the shape. Then spread it out and let your child try, as folding may be difficult.

 Learn how to play on page 64.

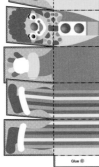

1 Cut the thick gray lines.

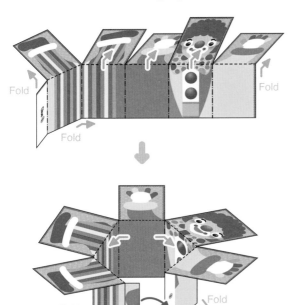

2 Fold the clown's body and glue the edges together.

Complete

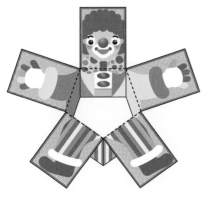

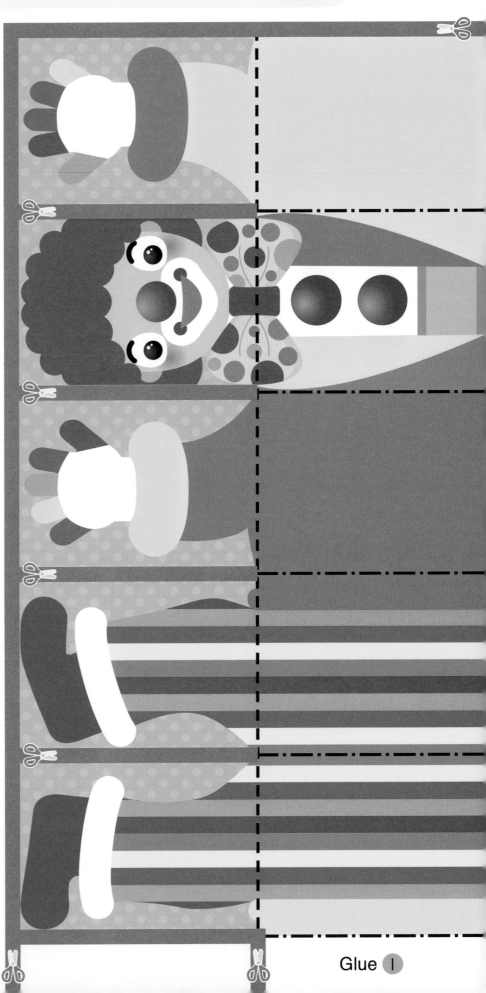

Glue Ⓛ

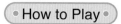

Move the clown to make him dance!